Anomaly

Mary F McDonough

GADFLY

First published 2020
Gadfly Editions

British Library Cataloguing in Publication Data
A CIP catalogue record for this book is
available from the British Library

ISBN 978-0-9928060-8-8 Paperback

Cover, design and typesetting by Martyn Clark,
Adobe Garamond Pro 11pt.

www.gadflyeditions.com
www.maryfmcdonough.com

First published 2020
Gadfly Editions

© 2020
Mary F McDonough

British Library Cataloguing in Publication Data
A CIP catalogue record for this book is
available from the British Library

ISBN 978-0-9928060-8-8 Paperback

Cover, design and typesetting by Martyn Clark,
Adobe Garamond Pro 11pt.

www.gadflyeditions.com
www.maryfmcdonough.com

Anomaly

Mary F McDonough

GADFLY

*Between when
and why,
there is void.
In void, becoming.*

Anomaly

When I had given up hope of
ever being me again, alive again,
something snapped.
I tore myself open.
Light came out.

I'm sewn back together.
All threads, crazy coloured knots,
zigzags, gaps.

I don't give birth to lies:
I adopt them,
swallow them whole
when they are disavowed.

They are almost always forgotten,
shoved in a corner,
when you've had your use of them.

I am the Mother of Lies.

I take them in
when all the inconsistencies
come home to roost,
bad-tempered starlings
squabbling in roof gutters
over what might be a bit of bark
or bread.

Dirty is bad. Dirty is good.
All a matter of context.
A dirty girl might be very good indeed.
A dirty whore—not so much.
Alliteration is the music of character assassination:
Slut. Slag. Slapper. Naughty. Totty. Hooker.
My personal favourite, age 5: Woman of the Night.
Streetwalker. Ho. Bad Girl.
Older words: Slattern. Trollop. Cunt. Doxy. Harlot.
Scarlet. Jezebel.
You. Me. Us.

You murdered me after I died. Skinless,
I'm like some hideous 1970s lava lamp,
transparent as squid—
my bones glow lurid red.

I repeat the words you said to me,
buoyed up on them like water,
until I run aground on the lies,
split open—a bag of skin.

Lies burn,
and taste of dirt and ash
in my mouth;
love tastes of chocolate,
and I ate your words
before I knew that you were lies.

Before I knew that you weren't mine.
I can remember how you tasted when you
were mine, the smell of your skin,
the way your breath burned.

I wanted to be consumed:
all that's gone now, all that hope and desire.
I am left with this cold fire,
and the taste of ash in my mouth.

I walk towards you, mouth open—
I could let all of the sex and sorrow
spill from my mouth into yours

> *pour la dernière fois.*
> *La dernière fois:*

a gift or a burden? I can't decide.
I carry myself *comme un verre*,
brimming over, yet not quite

> *maintenant, parce que*
> *c'est la dernière fois.*
> *Peut-être,*
> *c'est la dernière fois.*

I don't want to spill myself, to give
what you don't want

> *pour la dernière fois.*

I dance fitfully,
with regret—
we have never danced the way you danced tonight,
never loved as I would love you tonight,
and I'll never dance again, not really,

> *pour la dernière fois.*

Turning the compost heap
ensures it isn't too wet
or strong-smelling,
and that air gets in,
so that bacteria and other organisms
can colonise it.

A bag of skin
is not an ideal container.
Damp, stretchy, fertile ground
for all of the wrong things:
mildew, fungus, slime.

I was sure that we'd planted a garden.
Nothing growing here that I recognise.
No flowers that smell
of your skin, no petals
like your eyelids, pink darkening to
plum under your lashes. No sun
strikes through dank leaves
down into the roots.

There is nothing else
but this moment,
a thing we make and unmake
again and again
that might be love.

Lust for breakfast
sex for dinner
love for supper
throw away the bones of me after.

I can't see what follows:
there is only the bald
certainty, the urgency
of now, of you here with me.

An antidote to memory is called for.
Nothing else will suffice;
nothing else will ameliorate
available data that no longer applies.

Nothing is sure.
Grey sky and grey sea
meet.

No rhythm can be established:
snick–slap–clack.
Shale sliding underfoot.

I've picked up every stone on this beach,
Lifted and dropped them,
some more than once.
Gauged the weight of them,
Felt them:
smooth, rough,
wet, dry,
algae–slick.

None the right shape,
None will fill the space.
It needs to fit exactly.

I thought you broke my heart—
but all there is is emptiness.

Pond dipping.
Hopeful nets in,
rotten leaves out.
Disappointing.
But microscopic war
rages in our bucket.
Daphnea pursued
by nymphs' serrated jaws.

Swallow this.
You'll never have to think for yourself again.
It will make everything easier:
you won't try to get away,
and he can play you on his line.

Look at this. Your contract.
Write your name here.
Give it to him,
and you'll know what to do
for the next 50 years.

Do you think it is easy,
being nothing,
carrying nothing?

Shame is the mass of absent stars,
burnt-out suns,
dust without the Big Bang,
black-holed lifelessness stretching out.

Empty days.
Empty life.
Waiting.

I bloom with
strange fruit.
It changes—
lemon,
pear,
small orange,
grapefruit,
watermelon.

Tumours bloom
in other people,
in the same strange way.

I watch as he slices the skin from the ginger root. Meticulous. Focussed. I imagine his hands, but not the knife, moving down my body with the same care and precision. Fuck it. I'll just imagine the knife, delicately tracing an indentation down my body, never sliding in.

I take a sip of the infusion, and feel the warmth seep into me, as his eyes devour my face.

My lovelies,
so slim and shiny.
Care hasn't worn you out,
nor work stained you.

I polish and dry,
put away,
keep you safe.

I expect nothing from you,
but there is something you could do for me—
a small something—
slide between my ribs,
bleed me,
stay with me.

Sing me to sleep,
pretty knives.

We don't sleep;
we spoon in silence,
legs twined in mockery of love.
Your anger beats against me:
a second heart.

It pushes into me,
a letter opener thrusting its way into a letter
that feels like it was written for someone else.
Red words that aren't for me.

I leak through the hole
in the wall of us—

Before I went to hydrotherapy, I had imagined
rows of zombies in sensible black bathing suits
and bathing caps, dutifully bobbing up and down
to orders shouted through a megaphone by a
thick-bodied Physio named Libby. I expected
pain. Hypothermia. Torture. Calisthenics. Lots of
people eyeing other people up, trying to determine
their relative ranks in the Cripp Pecking Order.
But there weren't many of us. The water was
warmer than I'd expected. And no one shouted
anything. I felt the Dead Leg shift as I went
down the stairs, until I was standing, chest-deep,
and he floated away behind me like a rudderless
boat. He is always disobedient, but not usually,
obviously so: everyone waited patiently for my leg
to cooperate, and for me to force it back down
so my foot touched bottom. The Dead Leg kept
floating away, sometimes left, sometimes right,
enjoying the current created by other swimmers.

I drive home late from work.
Past the prison,
headlights skimming brick
and coiled razor ribbon wire.
I cross the bridge,
water almost dark enough to breathe.

I could be different.
I could open the door
and sink through the pavement,
let the water slough away
my too-human skin.

Remade, I would be a fleeting thing
with pebble eyes, worn from seeing.
I could be as cold as the river.

Maybe then you'd slide into me,
or drink me dry, before
I spill through your hands,
spill through your hands
between your fingers
and spatter on the ground—

You balance on my palm.
You've shrunk, lost all your water.
You sift inside your cardboard box.
It holds you together, now your skin is gone.
Ash, bits of teeth, the odd fragment of femur
trickle as I tip you from side to side.
I don't know what to do with you.

Should I put you on the passenger seat?
Gently buckle you in?
Talk to you as I drive?
Comment on the neighbour's chrysanthemums,
ask if you feel the weather changing?
A box doesn't seem like enough protection.
I'd prefer to sprinkle you in running water,
so you can't return.
I have no funerary offerings;
your lipsticks are all at home.
I don't want to put you down in the dark.
But the hole is here,
and the priest is impatient:
he's got another two boxes today.

I have been the shape of water. You will tell me
water has no shape of its own. I will tell
you that you are right. You will tell me
water is nearly formless, boneless.

I won't disagree. I flowed to fill, to complete
whatever container was offered. Indiscriminate.

Bones, spread out thin, a film over the bottom of
a trough, not enough of me to deepen or extend,
molecules barely touching, bonds stretched to
the point of evaporation. Condensation. Stasis.

*Don't do it. That's insane. The pier is one giant splinter. There
could be jellyfish. Or sharks. Or someone fishing, with a long
line. You could cut yourself. You won't be able to see. It's dark as
hell out there. No.*

> *Are you trying to tell me to stay out of the water?
> Out of the ocean? Just because it's dark? That's bullshit.*

*Why? I don't fucking get it. What do you get out of swimming?
You could die out there. You could get sucked right down by the
undertow and no one would find your body.*

> *I'll go because the ocean is here. I'm right here. I've never
> been in the Atlantic after dark. I won't be out there
> long. Seriously—are you my mother?*

The Undertow. Always in capital letters, hushed tones,
the same way people talk about cancer or alcoholism. *The
Undertow will get you. Bite into you. Pull you down.* It can
have me. I grab a towel. I change into my bathing suit.
Laurie asks if I'm going in. I run past her. My feet drum
along the boardwalk. I get splinters; I don't care. Much.
God, David is so irritating when he's right. I can feel the
thrum of the surf through my feet, shouting through my
bones. I decide, because Laurie dares me, to strip off. I
throw my suit and my towel onto the sand and sprint down
the beach. Straggling along behind me, I watch as a clump
of other people, led by Laurie, shuck their towels and
clothes. I'm so far away, backing into the surf, that I can't
tell who they are.

The wind is wild. The hurricane that has been predicted for
weeks may be arriving on the Outer Banks. I don't care. I
dive in, porpoising out, back in again, riding the waves back

to the beach. The sand the surf carries scrapes along my skin like a giant tongue; maybe The Undertow is a cat. I think about swimming out, straight out, towards the flickering lights of the shrimping boats. I decide to swim parallel to them, along the coast. I have no one to swim with; no one to play with. I'm fizzing with energy, and my skin is melting with the force of it. I'm just water, myself. Nothing solid, nothing human is left of me, other than frustrated lust. The water strokes me everywhere, and I wish The Undertow were human, or whatever it is I am.

I come back in after everyone else has retreated back into the kitchen. I lock myself in the bathroom, listening for a second to the beginning of a drunken argument before pinching my nipples and fingering myself with both hands until I'm shaking and exhausted.

The next morning my hair crunches on my pillow, stiff with salt, salt I can taste on my lips. I rummage in the bathroom cabinet for tweezers, tending to my feet, before hobbling to the door to taste the rain.

Some burn all the way down,
no matter how long we chew them,
or how well—
robot jaws working frantically.
Memories are just so much
blood, bone, gristle.

When she talks about the babies she's lost, I imagine a room full of tiny, transparent floating ghosts in diapers, playing with their toes as they bob around in the draft from the open door. Mom was always depressed about the missing babies, wondering if they would have had my Grandpa's smile or Aunt's eyebrows.

Sister Fidelis talked about a very different place where *little almost-angels* were stored like rolls of wallpaper on a shelf: *Limbo*. Men who'd committed suicide were kept there too, perpetually in karmic storage. Not-born leads to not-baptised, which equals *stained with Original Sin*. Murdered selves lead to unblessed burials outwith churchyards, perpetually stained with their own blood. The God who'd made Limbo, and the rules, frightened me more than the Devil.

Two trips to the principal's office later, I still refused to do my homework assignment: finding out the number, names, and genders, if known, of the miscarried not-quite-brothers-and-sisters our family could claim as their own almost-angels. I couldn't ask Mom, and Sister Fidelis had no right to know. I remembered that one of the babies had been named Patrick after he died, and was lost, and thought about him as I scrubbed the steps.

I was supposed to be a boy named Patrick.
I was supposed to replace the one she lost
before me, and maybe even others before
that. I became the whipping-boy instead.

I stand by the pond, eating wooly snow from my mitten.
The ice has thawed, and frozen again, but I can still see
the cracks. I don't know where the pond skaters go when
water freezes: there's no water here to keep them up,
scooting along, no fish pushing up against the top of
the water like the lid on a pot.

The house smells of good things. I pull my boots off,
and leave them dripping on the rug in the hall. Nanny
doesn't mind about drips; she mops them up, 'cause *a little
water never hurt anything*. The table has a crack that runs
across it. I help her pull it wide so we can drop leaves inside,
and pretend the table is bigger, and there are always so
many people here for dinner—like the old days, when
there weren't any missing uncles or grandads.

Potatoes don't have eyes any more after Nanny is through
with them. They lie flat, on the side of my plate, beached
in gravy. She glares down the length of table, passing
the rolls, and almost–arguments go out like candles.
Ideology has no place here: only butter, pepper.

You are up late, again, not sleeping, again. I don't know where Dad is. I hear the *brrrrr thunk click brrrrr thunk snip bbbbrrrrrrrrrrr*. Your wheezy sewing machine and dull scissors sing about a dress I won't want to wear. I hear your pursed-lips tuneless whistling, the same sound you make when you scratch hubcaps, going around corners too fast in the station wagon. You push the cloth under the biting needle, pulling steadily on the other side. The needle flashes up and down.

Tomorrow, I'll be choked by lace, suffocated under flounces, shouted at for wiggling, and slapped for getting the dress dirty.

What can I buy with my body, my sanity, if I let you use me as landfill? Become your oubliette, your disowned place of forgetting? Become my own holocaust? I know what girls should do. Girls should stop being girls. Stop feeling. Stop moving. *Be good, don't get the belt. Be good, don't get the belt. Be good, don't get the belt.* I chant it over and over: those words don't work against this blackness. I am not old enough to know what I am bargaining away. *20 like a man, or 40 like a girl? No girl is ever good enough.*

Maybe it would be better to never know what I am losing, every time I take my 20 like a man. There's nothing else for me to choose, other than to let him and the rest of them destroy me.

I will not hide
this strange purple number.
People don't like to see it.
You can touch it if you want.
It won't burn you.

No, it doesn't hurt;
that hurt already happened.
It reminds me that the worst
thing has already happened to me,
to all of us.

The worst things start with numbers.

6 million, perhaps 7.
I was 12.
No one else in my family survived.

One. Two. Three.
Breathe.
One. Two. Three.
Breathe.

I scythe through the water,
faster and faster,
as I turn my head left,
and then right,
every three strokes,
to snatch a lungful of air.

I can see my Mom. She's a tiny speck of red on the beach, flapping the sand from our towels. I'm jumping off of Dad's shoulders, into yellow-green water. I've never seen the ocean, for real, just pictures in *National Geographic*. Dad waves me toward the beach; he's talking.

I shout *crap crap crap crap CRAP* in my head as I dive down to touch the sandy ripples under my toes. I feel wild. I never want to get out of the ocean. Ever.

I'm under the waves, with my eyes open. I'm watching small fish drift past, clumping together, then zooming apart. I fly underwater with them, feeling the waves roar. My legs stretch behind me, and I cup the water with my hands. I roll and roll until I'm a selkie. I sprout fur, so I can stay out here forever.

Out of the corner of my eye, I see a something shiny. My brain screams *SHARK*. Just like in *National Geographic*. Something nearly as long as me, thin and blue-grey in the water. I don't want to, but I change back, and I'm a girl again. I try to swim faster. I can't keep looking. I don't stop to breathe, until I'm up on the beach, sprinting across the sand.

I don't notice until I sit down that I have lost the top of my bikini. I am almost naked in front of loads of grownups and kids and strangers. I'll get in trouble. I can't see it anywhere, so I cover my nipples with my hands.

My mother grabs my arm and pulls me up hard; one of my feet is almost off the ground. *You should be modest. You should be ashamed. Running like a wild animal, losing your top.*

I know what modest means, sort of: I should not want to be naked, fast, a selkie being licked by the ocean. Mom pinches me under my hair, pushing my chin up with her other hand. *Thank the boy. Thank the boy who brought you your bikini top. Now, Mary Frances.* I can't. I'm crying, and my voice doesn't work, and he's a *teenager.* He rubs my hair, puts the bikini top in my hand, and walks away.

My skin is being licked, all over my body.
Arms, legs, stomach, my face:
all being licked by something
gigantic and impersonal.

It knows me, but I don't remember it.

Dab your fingers in.
Don't leave them there too long,
or the font will get dirty as a bird bath.

Remember to use your right hand,
or Sister will hit you.
Father.
Son.
Holy Spirit.
Up and down, then left to right.

Leave Mary out of it altogether.

You are speckled.
Every freckle,
every blot of ink on paper,
or on your hand,
is a sin.

Do you understand?

Like stepping on lines,
stepping on cracks,
breaking your Mother's back,
sins are things you do on purpose,
leaving marks
you can't erase.

Your pattern wheel leaves blue-smudged tracks
on my hand. I drive it across my palm,
rewriting in chalk pinpricks.
My life line, bisected by dots and dashes,
judders. I'm sure my heart squeezes,
skips, as the blade of your scissors *snick snick snicks*,
biting through fabric, scraping along the table.
Am I the same girl I was before?
Am I real or imaginary, here or not here?
You tell me to stop getting the dust everywhere.

No one can climb as high as me. I can shin two stories up the roof-pole, and reach up to throw down chalky rocks for everyone. We can play Hopscotch right now if I get to the top. I'm a monkey, pushing up hard with my knees and heels. I'm taller than JJ at the top of the slide; he's waving and shouting but I can't hear him. I'm laughing and laughing. *CLANG.*

Sister Catherine is banging hard on the pole. *Dirty girl! Get DOWN. Now. Everyone can see your underwear. I've already called your mother!* I almost fall as I slide down, burning my legs and my hands on the paint. My mom is angry, when she comes to pick me up, because my uniform skirt is covered in chalk, and she'll have to wash it.

Today is going to be slow, like the last bit of toothpaste coming out. It always hurts my fingers, but I can't waste toothpaste or I'll get the belt. *Everything costs money.*

Going to play with the twins after school is fun. I feel grown up leaving with their Mom instead of mine. And they have dolls, Barbies and other ones, and I can take their shoes off and change their clothes.

Barbies don't ever wear hand-me-downs that are itchy and too big. They don't wear school uniforms or things that are ugly colours. Not like me. Momma says *new clothes are expensive and your cousins' clothes still have plenty of wear left in them,* but I don't care.

It's First Friday, so there's church today and no Reading Time. I wonder the whole way through mass what that word on the wall of the bank means. I'm sure it is bad. But I still think I know how it sounds. F U C K. Dangerous. Pointy. Important. I can't ask Sister cause she'll just send me to talk to Father Tom, but I'll ask Mrs. Gonzales.

Its cold out here. I'm waiting in the front yard for my Mom to come. Mrs. Gonzales says I'm a *dirty, bad girl and the twins won't associate* with me. Which means we can't play. She called my Momma and told her to come get me. The twins are sad, and they make their sad Barbies wave to me through the glass when their Mom isn't looking. I think they're still my friends.

They look like their Mom: long black hair, beautiful brown skin. Not like me. I don't look like my Momma: no black hair, no green eyes, way too many freckles. Sometimes the twins draw on my arm and connect the dots, but they don't make a secret picture. Freckles are like being bad. My skin is mostly white; I'm mostly good, but being bad even one time is so bad that it cancels the goodness out, like one freckle. I wasn't really cursing, not like the witches in the book who make people die or fall asleep by saying magic words.

My Momma isn't happy that I can read. She keeps making me tell her ingredients from the cookbook while she's stirring. I don't get to play here, either.

I'm a slattern, really.

The window is filthy, light limned in coal spores.
I cry, I bleed soot, perched on joists:
memories gather under eaves and in corners.

> *Maybe I should sweep.*
> *Each thought could spawn triplets.*

A good wife would scry past and future,
tucking them gently between sheets of white tissue.
I beg them to stay, offer them boxes.
I don't have anything else.

> *Someone might need you.*
> *Or the suitcases.*

No zippers, no buttons. Did you think this
would be easy? Mammals don't work that way.

Burn off all the hairs; don't singe the skin.
Measure twice, cut once. There's just the one
skin; you can't start over. Reserve it until step
10. Place carcass in the pot. Cover with water.
Boil until the bones move freely. Allow to dry.
To reassemble: joint with wire; splint with wood.
Experiment with lifelike poses.

When finished, contour and seal with clay. Insert
eyes. Replace skin; sew firmly closed. If you've
taken proper care, my seams won't show.

I don't watch Kojak on my TV; there are too many guns. I don't watch Starsky, either, or Muhammad Ali, even when he wins. Everyone gets too angry. I know Starsky isn't real—he's not like Mister Wilson. Mister Wilson is yours, but I don't think you want him any more, and he's always angry, and he shouts until I close the door.

You remember Brian, because he's your boy. When Mister Wilson shouts, Brian and I lean against the door, and we pretend he isn't real. That's my idea; I'm older than Brian, so I tell him it. I thought of an eraser I can see in my brain that lets me wipe away scary things. Brian decides to have a red eraser.

You come in after Mister Wilson leaves. I know you've been crying. I hug you, and smell your perfume. You laugh: my snuffling tickles your neck. Your happy feeling shines out of you, like a light, and I'm warm. You let me spray the perfume bottle by myself. Our secret. Momma told me *don't waste Marsha's perfume.* I lie and say I didn't. Using Chanel number 5 is a Bad Thing: I would get in trouble. But really I don't think it is wasting it anyway, just using it. My bubble feeling inside starts to shrink, the way it always does when I make a mistake. Learning to lie is my first secret.

My second secret is about Barbie. She has pink shoes and a
wedding dress. She can't stand up by herself; she has stupid feet.
Barbie teaches the wrong values, Momma says. Barbie is a little bit
Brian's, but really she's mine. I play with her every time I come
over to your house.

Brian plays with Ken, just to be nice because you said to, cause
he can play with her later. But not after his Dad comes home,
or Brian will get the belt for being a girl instead of a boy. I don't
tell Mister Wilson, even though he's Brian's Dad. Making Mister
Wilson angry is a Bad Thing. That lie is my third secret. I squeeze
my lips tight, and shake my head no when he grabs my shoulder
and shouts *did that boy play with that damn doll?*

I don't love Mister Wilson. I love you and Brian. I just feel a bit
sad for Mister Wilson. I wonder if I will have to tell Father Tom
about that lie when I'm bigger and I do Confession. I wonder if
God has a clipboard like the one I see in my head, getting fuller of
black X marks every time I lie.

Mister Wilson doesn't like playing. He doesn't like sharing you
with Brian or me or anyone. He thinks love is little, like a cupcake,
and he won't get enough if you share yourself with anyone else,
even a baby. Brian says that's why you can't have another baby. We
both know that's a dumb idea, cause love grows bigger inside of
you and spills out to other people every time you get happy. That's
the bubble feeling. I could float away.

My fourth secret is pink. Pink lips. I said it was Koolaid. Really
it was lipstick, pink lipstick the exact same color as Barbie's shoes
that never stay on. The lipstick is yours, but it is really a bit mine
too. I keep it in the drawer with your makeup. I love opening the
drawer and looking at it. Our secret. Everything in the drawer is in
rows, and I don't even know what lots of stuff in the drawer is for.

Brian and I don't like to play house. We are way too busy. We
have pencils and lists. I have your tall shoes and blue dress with

tiny straps. Brian has a shirt and a tie. We drink coffee and then we leave for work. He wants to come to my office, 'cause its at the top of the skyscraper. I say no. I'm busy with a project and my office is private. My purse is really yours too, and it is full of notes and curlers. Brian pulls Barbie's hair and I scream, because her head comes mostly off. I can see inside of her. Her head is empty, she is empty, and she isn't real. I feel sad for the rest of the day. You rub my back, and tell me I'm beautiful. I believe you, until it's time for me to go home. I'm only just me again then.

On another day, you drop Brian off at my house. I don't want to play with him here. It isn't the same. At your house, I'm special. I'm special because I'm me when I'm with you. You said girls can be anything they want, even if they want to be angry or fast or strong. Here, though, I just have to be good. And good means quiet. Good means not fussing about having my hair scraped back so tight it hurts. *Pride has no pain*, Momma says, and besides, *we have to keep it out of your eyes*. Long hair is like a disguise. It might even be a kind of a lie, cause you can look different every time. I don't want you to go. You are sad. I'm worried, and all you tell me is *I'm fine Mary Frances, I'm fine, I'll see you soon*. I try to believe you, but I think you have a secret without me in it.

Later, Brian and I brush our teeth. He's going to sleep at my house until you come back. Momma says Marsha and Mister Wilson are going to talk. I don't think its a good idea. He's too black and angry inside, and I can see his screams filling him up. Momma tells me *hush!!* I try to go to sleep like a good girl, but there's shouting.

Someone let your Mister Wilson into my house, and he's holding my baby Eddie like a football, screaming for Momma to give him Brian. She won't. Momma says *please let him sleep; he's so little, please don't do this*, and she climbs Mister Wilson and yanks Eddie away. My Daddy comes inside, shaking his head.

He was looking for something in Mister Wilson's car. No one can see me: I'm watching, like it's my TV, only I can't stop it. Eddie is screaming. Mister Wilson runs out the front door, covering his ears. Momma sees me, and tells me go back to bed. I hear her asking Daddy if he found the guns. He tells her *shut up*. He grabs me and rushes me back to my room. He calls someone. I'm afraid.

I wake up later and it is still dark. Brian is crying, but he's not in my room. He's in the living room, with a Grandma and a Grandad I don't know. They are taking him away. They are crying. Momma is crying. Momma tells me you and Mister Wilson are dead. She doesn't tell me how. She sends me back to bed. I cry, by myself, and that's my secret.

The next morning, I imagine you, head hanging to one side, like my secret Barbie when Brian pulled her head mostly off. Someone told my Momma he'd shot you there. More than one time, she thinks, because her husband said so, and *wasn't it just awful that Marsha was leaving Wilson and had a man on the side. On the side* is a weird thing; I don't know what it means, and I feel cold.

I was invisible: no one knew I heard her. I don't want to never come over to your house again. I didn't want to think about holes in your face. I try to rub the picture out with my eraser, but that just makes me think about bashing erasers at school with Brian. It's our favorite job. I will just say "no", when Mrs. Meyer asks me if I want to clean the erasers.

Someone closed your eyes, and closed the lid. A lady said they had a closed casket because Mister Wilson shot you, and you looked disgusting. Like the meat in our freezer, I think, smoking when the warm air comes in after I open it, all squashed and bony.

The funeral parlor man put your box on a conveyor, like the suitcase thing at the airport where I get my Daddy's suitcase. Then the fire ate your face. I wonder if it still had blood on it, or if someone washed you first. I hope they washed you first, 'cause you didn't like to *look a fright*. My Momma's friend says *nothing will be left of her but ashes and some bits of teeth*.

Another lady said *Marsha got what she deserved*. That's a lie. I don't tell any of them I can see their lies, rolling around inside of them, puffing out of their mouths and filling the room. They can't hear me anyway. I'm angry, but no one sees it. They tell each other I don't understand. I just keep sticking Lego together, trying to make a wall, but I don't have enough.

I wasn't brave. I'm frost inside, and people can see straight through me like I'm not here. I gave up. I turned off my light. I'm not clever or beautiful any more. But you still are, inside my head.

My Grandma says they are *dirty*. But I don't understand, because Momma lets them come live with us in our house. My other granny doesn't say that; *unlucky* is what she says. We let them live in our house, and they get their own room, those pregnant girls who came from someplace else. I like talking to them, and some of them let me read stories to them: I shout into their lumpy bellybuttons just in case the babies can hear, and they laugh, and that knocks me off their laps. I can hear them rocking in the rocking chair late at night when they can't sleep. Regina says that she tries to rock her baby to sleep so she can get some rest from the kicking and squirming. Regina had a boyfriend, but she doesn't any more. He didn't want to be a Dad.

What I don't understand is, if these are dirty, bad teenager girls, then why do they take care of me, and cook with me, and help Momma make dinner? Why do they eat with us at the table? My Daddy says *if you ever come to me like that, I'll beat the shit out of you and throw you back out onto the street, and you can work your way through life on your back.* Sex with someone who didn't marry you is a sin. It's a bad sin. But a girl who couldn't keep her baby gave Eddie to us, so how could she be bad? I love Eddie. Eddie is my best thing. I like watching him sleep, and when he turns over, his sweaty curls blop into his cheek.

I asked Grandma why she said the girls were dirty. She said they were sinners, and they would have to work very hard for *The Lord* to forgive them. None of them are mean to Grandma, so I don't understand why she hates them. I told my Momma, and she said sometimes people have mixed feelings about things. I always love the girls who come to stay with us, but sometimes I feel jealous, because then they are the oldest child and not me any more. I guess that's a mixed feeling. I hope I'm not dirty by accident when I'm older.

I'm in my room again, crying. Because you brought me back. I just wanted to live with you, but you brought me back. You pretended I met you outside, like I was just waiting for you to get here. You said we would talk about it the next time I come to your house, but I wanted to come today. I told you. I ran away.

I know Mister Wilson is angry every day. I know he hits. That happens to me in my house already. I'm good all the time. I try my hardest to behave. But I still got ugly sandals for fat feet today, just like Nancy's. I hate having things the same. I don't think the same or look the same. I can't be here, I can't go to your house, and everyone else I love is far away.

I'm running away. I don't want a snack, or my hairbrush.
I don't have to go very far—just to Marsha's. Brian said its
ok to come to their house. I saw a boy running away on my
TV. He packed things in a bandana, but I don't have one. I
got a paper Piggly Wiggly bag from the pantry for my stuff.
I'm not even scared about leaving. No one will notice I'm
gone, except maybe Eddie. I don't know how much babies
can remember. My good feelings are squeezing out, like my
toothpaste when I mash the tube against the sink.

I'm hurting like a dark bruise, inside. It's not like getting
a cut: my leaking isn't stopping. The black inside of me is
getting bigger, and my light is going to go out unless I leave
here. Good feelings make the light grow. When I have good
feelings, my light dances down to my toes and back up
again, like when I'm running, or when I get in the pool. My
light helps me float, and think good dreams instead of bad
ones. But the dark feeling is taking too many bites of my
light, and I can't stop it.

I was feral. Naked
as often as I was allowed—
oftener, really.

No shoes. No shirt. Climbing.
Hanging upside down from branches,
feeling my hair swirl in the wind.

And there was always wind. Always dust:
that's all West Texas is, one long dusty corridor
between nowhere and nowhere else on Earth.

If you count a mississippi, you are counting a second.
That's what Jerry says. I'm trying to stay down for
more *mississippis* every day, so my lungs get bigger.
I let my air bubbles out, one at a time, so I can
stay down longer. If you let them all out in a rush,
you have to hurry up out of the water. *Thirty–
three mississippi. Thirty–four mississippi. Thirty–five
mississippi.*

But sometimes my counting gets in a bit of a hurry.
My words smush together—*for-y-four-mississippi-
for-y-five-mississippi-for-y-six-mississippi*—and I have
to push off the bottom hard with my feet to get up
to the top fast enough.

At the bottom of the pool, I'm by myself for a little bit. I can't really hear anything: just some shouting and splashing. Mr. Mike says fighting with the water won't work; you have to let it hold you, and move with it. He says the best way to go out of the water is to push your face up through it, gently, like the water doesn't want to let you go, and you don't really want to get out of the pool. I like being by myself down here.

I went wrong,
right from the beginning.
Wrong sperm.
Already en route to
becoming Mary Frances.

6 cells old,
already fucked.

The worst things
start with numbers,
and end with pretending.

When

Why

GADFLY
www.gadflyeditions.com

www.ingramcontent.com/pod-product-compliance
Lightning Source LLC
Chambersburg PA
CBHW021625270326
41931CB00008B/877